QUICK
STAINE
A BEGINNER'S INSTRUCTION

Written by	Photography
Randy Wardell	Randy Wardell
Judy Huffman	Judy Huffman

Text Editor	**Special Thanks**
Robert Huffman	Bruce Boyle
	Suzanne Dick
Pattern Designs	Mike Hacikyan
Randy Wardell	Bob Kirk
Judy Huffman	Howard Mandel

Cataloguing in Publication Data

Wardell, Randy A (Randy Allan),

Huffman, Judy A. (Judith Anne)

Quick Success Stained Glass: A Beginner's Instruction Guide

ISBN 0-919985-18-1

1. Glass craft. 2. Glass painting and staining.

3. Glass craft– Patterns. I. Huffman, Judy, A. II. Title

TT298.W374 1992 748.5'028'2 C92-094248-2

An excellent example of a Landscape Window executed in the copper foil assembly method, by the Louis C. Tiffany Studios, circa 1900.
Courtesy: The Corning Museum of Glass

Printed in Canada by Thorn Press Ltd

Published By:

Wardell
PUBLICATIONS

P.O. Box 480069 Fort Lauderdale FL 33348-0069 USA

E-mail: info@wardellpublications.com • Website: www.wardellpublications.com

PREFACE

There is a bit of magic in a glass cutter. A simple score enables precision control to break a sheet of glass. A skilled crafter, using a glass cutter, can shape and assemble dazzling glass colors and create beautiful art objects. The stained glass process has been called "painting with light" and that just about says it all.

We decided to write and design this book "*Quick Success Stained Glass*" to introduce everyone to the possibilities of this exciting craft. All aspects are covered from the basic tools, supplies and techniques to pattern making, glass scoring, breaking and soldering. Included are full-size patterns for sun catchers, window panels, lampshades among other projects all specifically designed for the beginning crafter, to get you up and running fast.

We are confident that this *Quick Success* book, along with the assistance provided by your instructor or local glass supplier, will get you on your way to creating the heirlooms of tomorrow.

From Wardell Publications book
Northern Shades - 985173

CONTENTS

CONTENTS

Egyptian cast and core formed glass vases from 18th -19th dynasty.
Courtesy: The Corning Museum of Glass

Pre-historic Glass Making

The exact turn of events in the history of glass making is difficult to ascertain. It was most likely refined in Egypt and surrounding regions, where the basic raw material, silica sand, was present in ample supply. Shards of glass unearthed in Egypt, Iraq and Saudi Arabia have been dated to as early as 7000 B.C. Early vessels were produced between 3000 and 1500 B.C. using a sand-core mold. Many centuries later the glass blowers "blowpipe" was developed and is still very much in use today, producing a desirable type of stained glass, called Mouth Blown Full-Antique sheet glass.

Mouth-blown Sheet Glass

To produce a flat sheet of glass in this time honored mouth blown method, molten glass is gathered on the end of a blowpipe and formed into a large ball by blowing and rotating the gather through a series of wooden molds. The ball is then finished into a cylinder by a master craftsman. While the glass is still red hot, the bottom is cut open, the blowpipe is removed, and both ends are enlarged to form a hollow cylinder. This cylinder is then split length-wise, placed into an annealing kiln, re-heated, and laid flat to create a sheet.

Modern Glass Making

The basic raw materials used to produce glass are silica or quartz sand, limestone, and soda potash. The colors are created by adding metal oxides to the batch. For example, gold oxide is added for ruby & pink, selenium for orange & yellow, and cobalt for blue, to name just a few. This mixture is put into a crucible furnace and heated to (+or-) 3000°F (1650°C). This extremely high temperature turns the solid raw materials into molten glass.

Colored glass is manufactured throughout the world by many companies. Some of them form sheets using the mouth blown method as described above.

Glass Development through the Ages

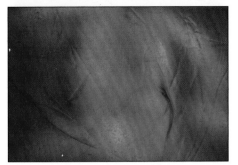

Modern Antique Glass

History

• An historic perspective is very important in helping us to understand how the art of stained glass crafting began and how it fits into our modern day civilization.

However, the vast majority use a roll-forming process. Some large factories have fully automatic sheet forming machines, while others use a low-tech hand-cranked approach. In either case, a base layer of molten glass is poured onto a steel table where other colors may be added and swirled together. The molten mixture is then sent through the rollers and formed into a flat sheet. It is finished by cooling in an annealing kiln.

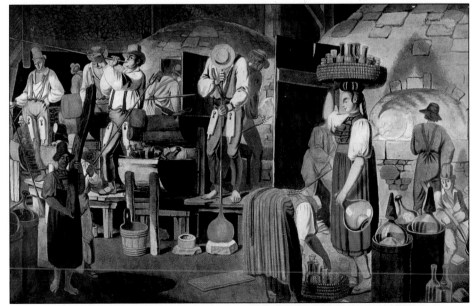

Aquatint of early 19th century glass making in the Black Forest 1820-1827
from Glashutte im "Aule" by A. Schreiber; Courtesy: The Corning Museum of Glass

Glass Definitions

• Learning to identify the various types and textures of stained glass will be a great asset when you are choosing glass at the supply shop.

• These photographs show only a few of the hundreds of colors, textures and styles of glass available today.

Solid Opalescent

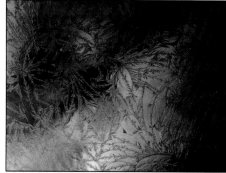

Glue-chipped Cathedral, Iridized

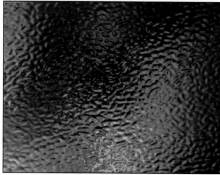

Muffle-back Cathedral

Today we are fortunate to have literally hundreds of glass types, styles, and surface textures to choose from. Manufacturers have developed unique varieties of glass textures and colors with their own special descriptive names, far too many to list here. However, to simplify the explanations, we can fit them all into three main categories.

• **Cathedral Glass:** This is a roll formed glass, very uniform in thickness, transparent or semi-transparent, and available in single or multi color mixtures. A combination of two or more colors is called a streaky cathedral. Often this glass is given a surface texture, which can range from granite or hammered effects to flowers or fern patterns. It can have small bubbles or large swirls within the glass, or subtle waves and

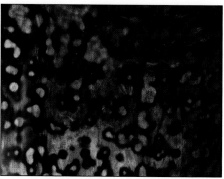

Ring-mottled Opalescent

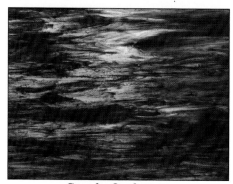

Streaky Opalescent

ripples reminiscent of water. Cathedral glass is versatile and inexpensive, prompting its use in a wide range of stained glass applications.

Drawn (or Fourcault) glass is a major sub-category of cathedral glass. Sometimes referred to as semi-antique, it has a uniform thickness, is quite transparent, and both sides are smooth and highly polished. Subtle hair-line striations add movement to this beautiful glass.

• **Opalescent Glass:** This glass is easily identified by a milky or opal-like appearance.

Opal glass is manufactured using the roll-forming process. It is available in a wide range of styles, from a solid single color to as many as 5 or 6 colors swirled and streaked throughout the sheet. Some sheets transmit little or no light, while others are semi-transparent.

When an opal color is mixed with a transparent cathedral color on the rolling table, the resulting glass is called wispy or streaky opal, depending on the ratio of the mix. With color and texture combinations numbering in the hundreds, opal glass is used extensively in windows, lampshades, and virtually every stained glass application.

From Wardell Publications book
Bevel Window Designs - 985076

From Wardell Publications book
Introduction to Stained Glass- 985041

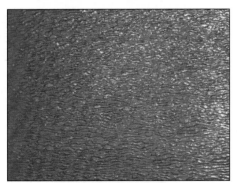

Ripple-back Cathedral

Fracture & Streamer Cathedral

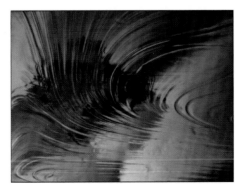

Reamy Cathedral

• **Full Antique:** Produced in the time honored mouth blown method, Full Antique features brilliant, transparent colors and a distinctive fire-polished finish. Typically irregular sheet thicknesses result in dark and light areas within a single sheet creating opportunities for shading and other subtle design possibilities. Full antique glass is generally more expensive than the roll formed cathedrals but the brilliant, rich colors add a special touch to many projects and are often worth the extra expense.

Flashed Antique is a major sub-category of Full Antique. This glass is created by gathering a base color of molten glass on the blow pipe, then adding a layer of a darker color before the blowing and shaping takes place. A finished sheet of flashed glass has a base of one color (or clear) with a thin layer of a darker color on one side only.

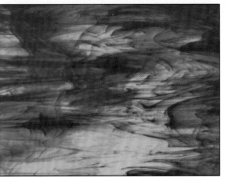

Wispy Opalescent

Granite-back Streaky Opalescent

Flashed glass is often etched by sandblasting to remove portions of the darker color, revealing the lighter color underneath.

You will find many variations within these three general categories. To help you become more familiar with stained glass, ask your supplier to identify and define some of the glass they carry, especially the ones you like. You will be able to refer to the glass by name the next time you are trying to describe exactly what you are looking for. (Just for fun, ask your supplier to show you an "iridized gold-pink wispy-opalescent ripple". They will be impressed).

From Wardell Publications book
Mirrors & Frames - 985157

Color Design and Harmony

Creative Decisions

• All Wardell Publications books and many other glass pattern books feature creative suggestions for each project. Glass color, type & texture, as well as a material list, accompany all the full-size patterns in this book. However, feel free to make your own creative decisions.

You need only speak the words "stained glass" to conjure up visions of exciting color and design in the mind of just about anyone. Stained glass artisans require two very different skills, commonly referred to as *Arts* and *Crafts*. The *Crafts* part is the physical hands-on construction of the project. The *Arts* part is conceptual and involves selection of the design and all related creative decisions. There are rules for color relationships to aid in some decisions. (see *Color Theory* on this page). However most creative decisions must be based on personal preference and artistic feel. Take your time, listen to advice, but learn to trust your own creative skills. The following set of guide lines may help with this critical task.

Plan - Before you visit the glass supply studio, color a small sketch of your design with pencil crayons or water paints. Make several copies in different color combinations until satisfied that you have achieved the desired creative effect.

Theme - Sometimes the design itself or the function of your project will dictate the color theme. First, settle on a color that will be dominant. Then complete the theme by building on this base color.

Balance - Stand back from your color sketch and analyze your color choices. Do they harmonize and flow across the entire design? As you look at the sketch try to get a feel for the overall color effect. Look for contrasts & blends, darks & lights – in a word, balance.

When you are confident of your color choices, you are ready to visit your local glass supply shop. There you will find a seemingly endless variety of colors, textures and types of glass. This can be intimidating. Start by picking the glass for your dominant color and build around it. Stay as true as possible to your final color sketch, but don't be afraid to ask for advice and recommendations.

Color Theory

The color wheel is a clever design tool which greatly simplifies many color decisions. There are three primary colors -Red, Yellow, and Blue. Between these colors are three secondary color mixes -Orange, Green, and Violet. In theory, the color combinations are limitless. The important thing to remember is that every color can be found somewhere on the color wheel.

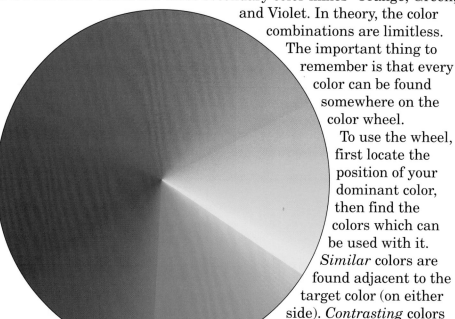

To use the wheel, first locate the position of your dominant color, then find the colors which can be used with it. *Similar* colors are found adjacent to the target color (on either side). *Contrasting* colors are 1/3rd of the way around the wheel (in both directions). *Complementary* colors are directly across the wheel (on the opposite side). For example, if you pick primary red as the dominant color in your project, then burnt orange & magenta would be similar colors, blue & yellow would be contrasting colors, and green would be a complementary color. Try using the wheel to do a color palette set for your favorite color.

From Wardell Publications book Bevel Window Designs- 985076

Think About Safety

The location and set-up of your home stained glass workshop is closely tied to safety. Everyone knows that glass edges are *extremely* sharp and are very dangerous, especially for children. If there are children in your home, it is strongly recommended that you make your glass studio inaccessible to them, including while you are working at your project. There are simply too many hazards involved for you to "just keep an eye on them". There will be slivers and shards of glass, a hot soldering iron, corrosive acid flux & patina, solder (which contains lead), tools, knives, and a grinder. All of these can cause serious injury at the blink of an eye. You must take responsibility, not only for your own safety, but for all those who may enter your studio. The most important advice to prevent injury is in fact an old adage: *A Place for Everything and Everything in its Place!* In other words, get your space organized with shelves, racks, and containers. Use them as a matter of habit. Don't leave things, *especially glass*, lying around. Put the lid on chemicals immediately after use, always place the hot soldering iron in the holder and always...

THINK ABOUT SAFETY!

A home glass studio can be either temporary or permanent. The following necessities are common to both.

• **An Electrical Outlet:** The preferred outlet is one with GFI (ground fault interrupter), or, at the least, a power bar with a grounded plug and built-in circuit breaker rated for a maximum load of 15 amps.

• **Good Lighting:** Natural light is the best but often that is not an option. A good alternative is a fluorescent fixture, and if you have a choice, get the full spectrum or daylight tubes for better color values. Another choice is to replace incandescent bulbs with screw-in fluorescent bulbs. They give a bright, soft light and save energy.

• **Work Bench:** The ideal height for a work bench is waist high. However, a standard height table with a protective covering will do just fine.

• **Work Surface:** You will need a workboard for glass cutting and project assembly. A piece of 1/2" (12mm) plywood 24" x 48" (.5m x 1m) or similar size is plenty for most projects. For glass cutting you might consider a Morton grid-top surface which adds a bonus of safety and has optional cutting guides and assembly jigs.

• **Tool Box or Tool Rack:** A standard chest-type tool box will hold the majority of your glass tools. In a permanent studio, put a pegboard behind the work bench and use the various hooks and racks available to set up an organized and handy display.

• **Glass Storage Box or Rack:** Heavy duty corrugated boxes can be modified to hold a small amount of glass. If you have a permanent space, the ideal solution is a custom built work bench and glass storage rack.

• Carefully read all workshop safety information.

• An important shop item is a portable workboard. A 1/2" (12mm) plywood 24" x 48" (.5m x 1m) is perfect.

• A standard chest type toolbox is handy for all your glass tools.

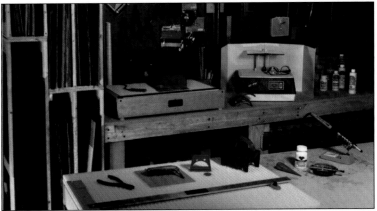
An ambitious home workshop

Think About Safety

Your studio should be in a room that does not have carpeting. No matter how careful you are, glass chips will fall to the floor and it is very difficult to get all of them out. If you have to use a room with carpet, cover your working area with a plastic carpet runner.

You will need some ventilation to pull the (mildly) toxic soldering fumes away from your face. A household fan blowing across your work area will work nicely. If possible, open a window (weather permitting) or use a fan which is vented to the outside.

- The purchase of a glass cutter is perhaps the most important tool decision you must make. Read the section on Self Lubricating Tungsten-carbide wheel cutters, the top choice for quick success.

- Purchase the highest quality cutter you can afford. It will save you money in the long run and be assured, you won't be sorry.

GLASS CUTTERS

Selecting your first glass cutter is an important decision. Experienced teachers know that the cutter you choose can often make the difference between quick success and total frustration. You must consider hand comfort as well as budget and anticipated frequency of use. Read the following descriptions and ask your supplier for their recommendation.

There are dozens of different cutters, all with their own unique qualities. All cutters can be divided into a few general categories commonly available in the stained glass industry.

- **Self Lubricating with Tungsten-carbide Wheel:** These cutters are by far the most popular among stained glass enthusiasts. They have a long lasting tungsten-carbide wheel with the added benefit of self lubrication. In most models, the handle of the cutter has a reservoir for the lubricant. Each time the cutter is used, a small drop of cutter oil is fed to the wheel. The lubricant is necessary to produce a quality score and to maintain a sharp wheel. The higher initial cost of this cutter will be quickly offset by lower accidental glass breakage.

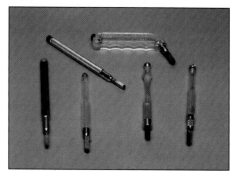

An assortment of Self Lubricating Tungsten-carbide cutters

- **Traditional Cutter with Standard steel Wheel:** These kinds of cutters are the least expensive and sometimes are referred to as "beginner" cutters due to the low cost. They are available in a variety of handle

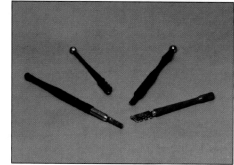

An assortment of Manual Lubricating cutters

shapes made of metal, wood or plastic and must be lubricated prior to each score. While they can produce a satisfactory score, it takes considerably more practice to master one of these cutters than one of the tungsten-carbide wheel models.

- **Carbide-steel Wheel:** The carbide-steel model is similar to the standard steel wheel cutter, but is slightly more expensive. However, because of the harder carbide-steel, the wheel stays sharp for a longer period of time.

- **Cutter Guides & Shape Jigs:** Your supplier will have a wide selection of special tools to assist in scoring circles, strips, and multi-angled geometric shapes, among others. These tools can be especially useful for quantity production work or when you are building a project which contains many repetitive shapes. Ask for a demonstration to see how one of these tools may benefit you.

From Wardell Publications book
Lampshade Patterns I - 985009

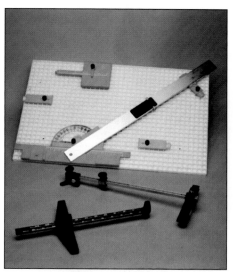

An assortment of Cutter guides & shape jigs

PLIERS

Pliers are an essential tool for working with stained glass. You will find a broad range in prices among pliers of similar style. Some differences are in the hardness of the steel, the precision of the jaw fit, or spring-action opening. Ask your instructor or supplier for their recommendations on pliers.

• Combination Breaker-grozer Pliers:

As suggested by their name, these pliers were designed for a double duty and will quickly become the most versatile "must-have" tool you own. They have one curved jaw and one flat jaw which meet only at the tip. Their primary function is to grasp the glass securely on one side of a score when breaking it apart. Both jaws have serrated teeth to assist in their other duty, called grozing, which involves removing small bits of glass from an irregular edge.

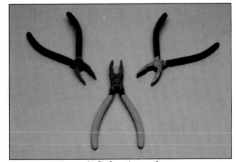

A Selection of
Combination Breaker-grozer Pliers

From Wardell Publications book
More Lampshade Patterns II - 985050

• Breaking Pliers:

The straight jaws on these pliers are designed to grasp the glass to assist in breaking it apart. The wide jaws meet only at the tip and are not serrated.

• Gripping Pliers:

These unusual shaped pliers are used exclusively to securely hold smaller glass pieces in a horizontal position while grinding. They allow easy access to the spinning grinder head, while keeping your fingers at a safe distance.

Breaking Pliers & Gripping Pliers

A Selection of
Score Running Tools

• Score Running Tools:

The majority of the tools in this category resemble standard pliers but are for a completely different function. These tools are designed to apply pressure to a score in a very specific way to force the break across the glass. The jaws may have a centering mark or a button which must be aligned with the score. When the pliers handles are squeezed, pressure is exerted from under the score, causing the break to run (follow) along the score line.

One brand of running tool is not a pliers style at all. Instead it uses a pressure bar and button system. It is available in full size or in a mini version made of lightweight plastic and attached to a cord, allowing it to be hung conveniently around your neck. Ask your glass supplier for a demonstration of score runners.

• Breaker-grozer pliers are the most essential and versatile pliers for stained glass crafting and are in the "must have" category. Read about them in the section, Combination Breaker-grozer.

• Score running tools are fast becoming essential. For more information on the "button fulcrum" category of breaking tools see this column on pages 15 & 16.

From Wardell Publications book
Terrariums & Planters - 985025

• A quality soldering iron and the ability to regulate the temperature are very important. See the section on Temperature Control Iron.

• Read "Think About Safety".

SOLDERING IRONS

Soldering is the act of melting an alloy (solder) to join metals, such as copper foil or came.

To sustain the proper melting temperature required for stained glass soldering, you will need an iron between 80 and 150 watts, preferably with some method of controlling the temperature. An iron which is too hot will risk cracking the glass, too little heat and the solder will not melt sufficiently for a smooth flow.

• Temperature Control Iron:

These irons are very popular among stained glass enthusiasts. Some models have a built-in rheostat for controlling the temperature. Others have internal mechanisms or a "variable tip controller" to fix and maintain a constant preset temperature. A steel-clad chisel-point tip between 1/4" (6 mm) and 3/8" (10 mm) is preferred.

• Standard Soldering Irons, (not temperature controlled):

It is generally accepted that a wand or rod-style iron is the best choice for stained glass crafting. Most soldering irons available for glass crafting fit into this non-temperature controlled category, however this can be easily rectified (see controller below). The iron should be at least 80 watts and have a steel-clad chisel-point tip between 1/4" (6 mm) and 3/8" (10 mm).

• Rheostat Temperature Controller:

A standard (non-temperature controlled) iron is connected to this device to regulate the amount of current the iron receives. Simply adjust the rotary dial to vary the maximum temperature the iron can reach.

*An Assortment of
wand or rod-style Soldering Irons*

• Soldering Iron Tips:

Iron manufacturers offer a variety of tips for their irons. A steel-clad chisel-point tip is recommended for glass crafting. Tips range in size from 1/8" (3mm) to 1/2" (13mm) and are interchangeable to suit the soldering task. Ask your supplier which size tip would fulfill your soldering needs.

*Soldering Iron Stands
with tip cleaner sponge*

*From Wardell Publications book
Bevel Window Designs - 985076*

• Soldering Iron Stand:

Most soldering iron stands have a steel coil holster mounted on a heavy cast metal base. Always place your hot soldering iron safely in the holster when your iron is at rest.

• Iron Cleaning Sponge:

The tip of your iron will tend to collect residue while you solder and should be cleaned off frequently. A heat resistant sponge, dampened with water, is effective and easy to use. Simply wipe the hot iron tip across the damp sponge periodically. Most iron stands have a built-in tip cleaner tray and sponge.

GLASS GRINDERS

Experienced glass crafters know that no matter how accomplished they become at glass scoring and breaking, some adjustment will be necessary for a precision fit of the glass pieces. A glass grinder makes this task seem almost effortless. These special machines are offered by several manufacturers, with models for occasional-duty to professional-duty. They feature a diamond embedded grinding head, which rotates in a reservoir of coolant. The coolant reduces chipping and helps eliminate harmful glass dust.

It is possible to enjoy glass crafting without a grinder. However, their use will instantly increase the quality of your work while reducing the frustration. Please ask your supplier for a glass grinder demonstration.

• **Diamond Grinder Heads:**
Interchangeable heads of various diameters, grits and shapes have been developed for specific functions. The standard grit of 100 mesh is preferred for most grinding tasks. A fine grit of 220 mesh and a coarse grit of 60 mesh are also available. The smaller diameter heads are for tight radius grinding, plus they have the added benefit of grit on the top end, which can be used to drill a hole in the glass.

Glass Grinder by Inland ™

Glass Grinder by Glastar™

Grinder heads & accessories

A professional grinder by Glastar ™

• A glass grinder will make project fitting quick and easy. Many stained glass shops have grinders available for use at their instruction classes and some day-rent grinders for a minimal cost.

• Read "Think About Safety" for eye protection.

From Wardell Publications book
Lampworks - 985149

From Wardell Publications book
Stained Glass Boxes - 985017

Tools of the Trade - Miscellaneous Tools

• This list is provided as a basic guide to the tools and equipment you will need to get started in stained glass crafting. You may already have several of these items around your home, so find what you can before heading to the glass supply center.

Essential Tools
• Glass cutter(see pg. 8)
• Glass pliers(see pg. 9)
• Soldering iron (see pg. 10)
• Workboard (see pg. 7)
• Lathekin/Fid
• Pattern shears
• Hammer
• Marking pens
• Push pins/Layout kit
• Drawing equipment
• Masking tape
• Safety glasses/Goggles
• Rubber gloves - household
• Bench brush/Whisk
• Tray & Brush for flux
• Straight Edge/Glass Square

Optional Tools
• Carborundum stone
• Foil dispenser
• Needle-nose pliers
• Fulcrum Breaker (see pg. 16)

• **Drawing Equipment:**
Pencil, eraser, ruler 18" to 36” (.5m to 1m), drawing paper (like the pages of this book), pattern card (like the cover of this book), carbon paper, square, and masking tape.

• **Straight Edge / Glass Square:** Use a yard (meter) stick or a glass square to guide your cutter on straight scores.

• **Lathekin / Fid:**
A lathekin or fid is used to burnish (flatten) the foil to the glass edges.

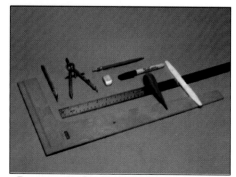

Drawing tools; Glass square; Lathekin; Fid; Craft Knife; Glass Pen.

• **Push Pins, Strips & Nails:**
You will need push pins, tape, small nails and wood strips to hold the glass while soldering.
A kit called the Layout Block System™ contains the items you will need for most projects.

Layout Block System™ mounted, with a pattern on a sheet of plywood.

• **Pattern Shears:**
The special triple blade design of these scissors automatically removes a narrow strip of paper while cutting the pattern template pieces. By removing this narrow strip, an allowance is made for the foil (or metal came). This also provides a margin for error in glass cutting & fitting. (see pg. 17 for photo)

Here is a short list of optional equipment that you may find useful in addition to the more essential tools.

• **Carborundum Stone:**
A coarse knife-sharpening stone can be used to remove rough edges on your glass pieces if you do not have a glass grinder.

• **Foil Holder / Dispenser:**
A foil holder conveniently organizes open rolls of foil and prevents them from becoming entangled while you are foiling.

Think About Safety

• Wear Safety glasses or goggles when scoring, breaking, grozing & grinding glass, and when soldering.
• Use a bench brush or whisk broom to clear away the glass chips from your work surface.
• Bandaids will be necessary to patch up even small nicks & cuts. ALWAYS cover those battle scars to keep flux, dirt, and especially lead (solder) out.

• **Hand Foilers & Crimpers / Foiling Machines:**
An assortment of devices to assist in copper foil wrapping are available. Some machines center and wrap the foil around the glass, others fold and crimp the foil. They are assistance devices and do not work automatically. With practice they can be useful.
Ask for a demonstration of the various foil wrapping aids to see if one might be of benefit to you.

Assorted Copper Foiling Aids; Lathekin; Fid.

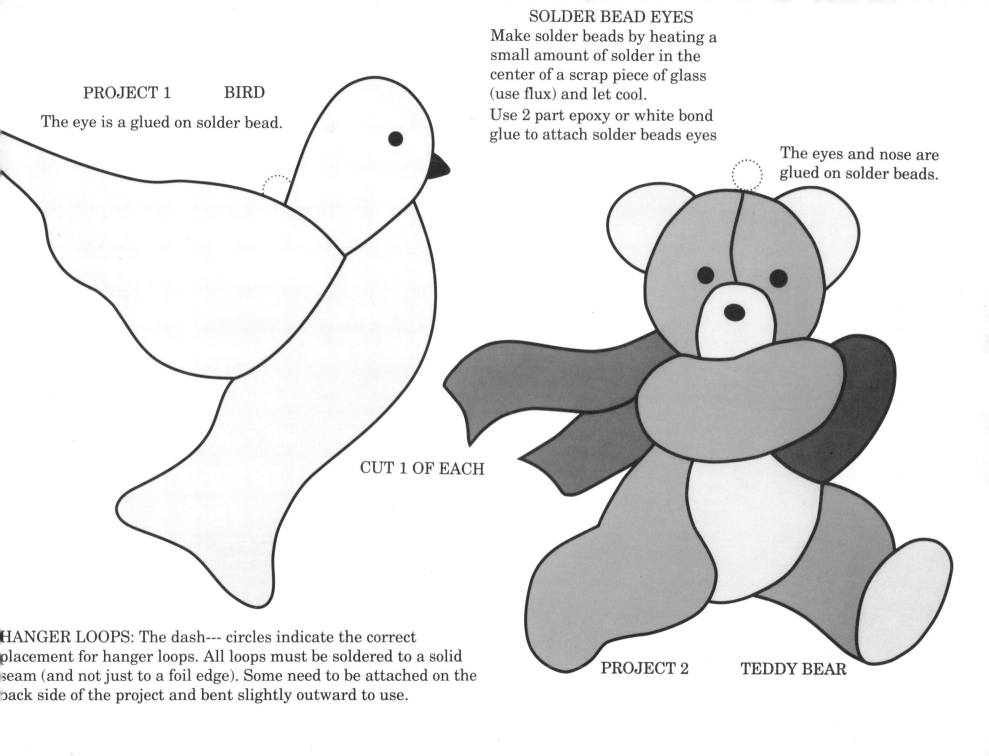

PROJECT 1   BIRD

The eye is a glued on solder bead.

SOLDER BEAD EYES

Make solder beads by heating a small amount of solder in the center of a scrap piece of glass (use flux) and let cool.

Use 2 part epoxy or white bond glue to attach solder beads eyes

The eyes and nose are glued on solder beads.

CUT 1 OF EACH

HANGER LOOPS: The dash--- circles indicate the correct placement for hanger loops. All loops must be soldered to a solid seam (and not just to a foil edge). Some need to be attached on the back side of the project and bent slightly outward to use.

PROJECT 2   TEDDY BEAR

Keep this copy as your original. Make copies for use as patterns

CUT 1 OF EACH

RAINBOW LANDSCAPE   PROJECT 15

PROJECT 9   BASEBALL FAN CLUB
CUT 1 OF EACH

Assembly Note:
Solder the bottom pieces
on your bench in a flat
disk shape. The petal cup
is raised into a cone (see
hint by project 12 & 13) and
soldered to the bottom at the
solder bead joint lines.

BOTTOM
CUT 6

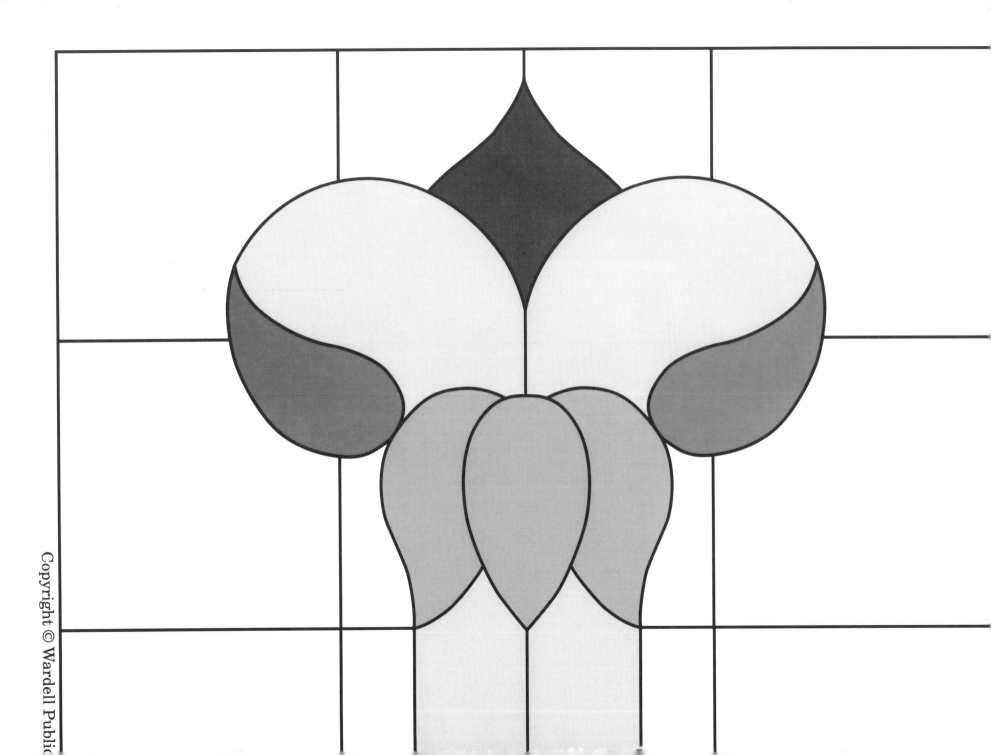

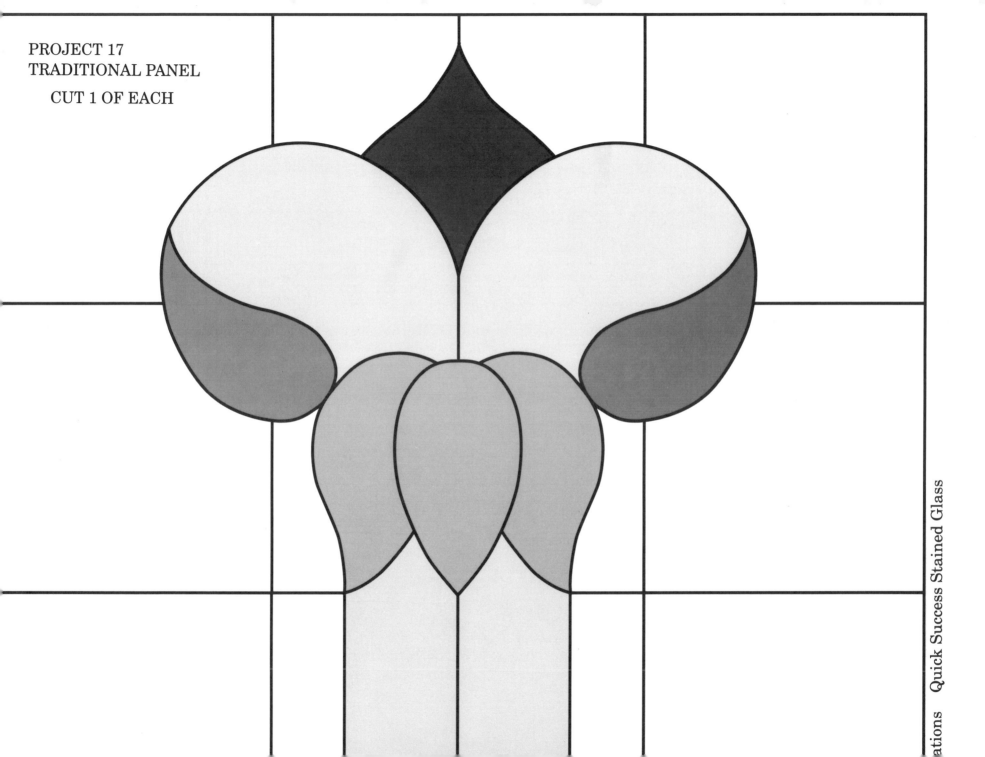

PROJECT 17
TRADITIONAL PANEL

CUT 1 OF EACH

CUT 1 OF EACH

PROJECT 7   MOTHER GOOSE
The eye is a glued on solder bead.

PETAL CUP
CUT 6

PROJECT 14   3-D DAFFODIL

How-To Insert the Joiner Piece

Joiner pieces are glass accents that span across an angled joint in any 3-D construction. They are tack soldered to the lampshade after the initial assembly is complete. First, check the joiner pattern piece to the space and adjust if necessary. Next, cut, clean & foil one glass piece. Position it into the space, so the edges are flush with the adjacent sections and tack solder it. Do not be too concerned if all edges are not completely flush since that is often not possible (or necessary). Check the pattern to the next joiner piece space and repeat the procedure for each joiner piece until all are installed. Finish the lamp assembly and bead solder in the normal manner.

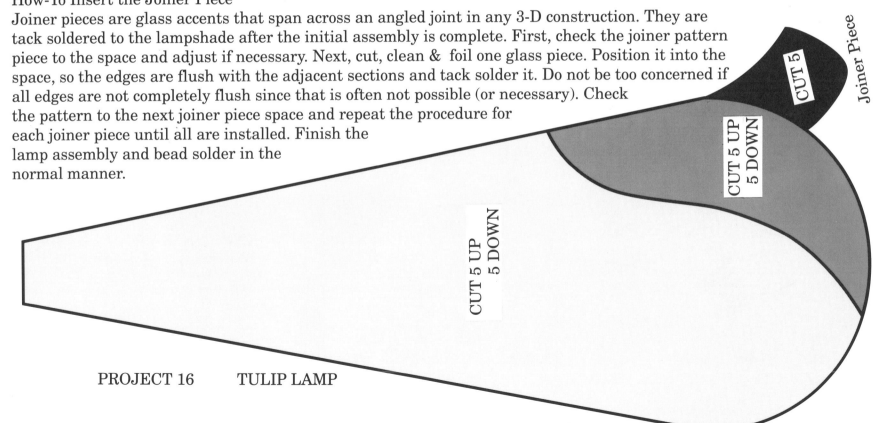

PROJECT 16   TULIP LAMP

Joiner Piece

CUT 5

CUT 5 UP
5 DOWN

CUT 5 UP
5 DOWN

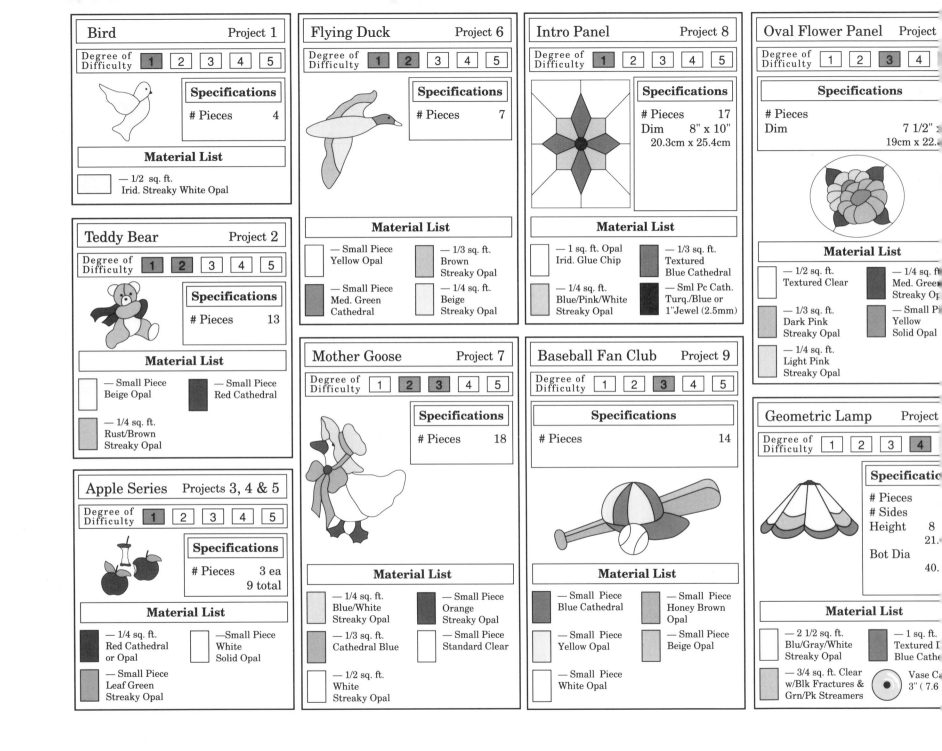

Bird — Project 1

Degree of Difficulty: **1** 2 3 4 5

Specifications
Pieces 4

Material List
— 1/2 sq. ft.
Irid. Streaky White Opal

Teddy Bear — Project 2

Degree of Difficulty: **1** **2** 3 4 5

Specifications
Pieces 13

Material List
— Small Piece
Beige Opal

— Small Piece
Red Cathedral

— 1/4 sq. ft.
Rust/Brown
Streaky Opal

Apple Series — Projects 3, 4 & 5

Degree of Difficulty: **1** 2 3 4 5

Specifications
Pieces 3 ea
9 total

Material List
— 1/4 sq. ft.
Red Cathedral
or Opal

—Small Piece
White
Solid Opal

— Small Piece
Leaf Green
Streaky Opal

Flying Duck — Project 6

Degree of Difficulty: **1** **2** 3 4 5

Specifications
Pieces 7

Material List
— Small Piece
Yellow Opal

— Small Piece
Med. Green
Cathedral

— 1/3 sq. ft.
Brown
Streaky Opal

— 1/4 sq. ft.
Beige
Streaky Opal

Mother Goose — Project 7

Degree of Difficulty: 1 **2** **3** 4 5

Specifications
Pieces 18

Material List
— 1/4 sq. ft.
Blue/White
Streaky Opal

— 1/3 sq. ft.
Cathedral Blue

— 1/2 sq. ft.
White
Streaky Opal

— Small Piece
Orange
Streaky Opal

— Small Piece
Standard Clear

Intro Panel — Project 8

Degree of Difficulty: **1** 2 3 4 5

Specifications
Pieces 17
Dim 8" x 10"
20.3cm x 25.4cm

Material List
— 1 sq. ft. Opal
Irid. Glue Chip

— 1/4 sq. ft.
Blue/Pink/White
Streaky Opal

— 1/3 sq. ft.
Textured
Blue Cathedral

— Sml Pc Cath.
Turq./Blue or
1"Jewel (2.5mm)

Baseball Fan Club — Project 9

Degree of Difficulty: 1 2 **3** 4 5

Specifications
Pieces 14

Material List
— Small Piece
Blue Cathedral

— Small Piece
Yellow Opal

— Small Piece
White Opal

— Small Piece
Honey Brown
Opal

— Small Piece
Beige Opal

Oval Flower Panel — Project

Degree of Difficulty: 1 2 **3** 4

Specifications
Pieces
Dim 7 1/2"
19cm x 22.

Material List
— 1/2 sq. ft.
Textured Clear

— 1/3 sq. ft.
Dark Pink
Streaky Opal

— 1/4 sq. ft.
Light Pink
Streaky Opal

— 1/4 sq. ft.
Med. Green
Streaky Op

— Small P
Yellow
Solid Opal

Geometric Lamp — Project

Degree of Difficulty: 1 2 3 **4**

Specificatio
Pieces
Sides
Height 8
21.
Bot Dia
40.

Material List
— 2 1/2 sq. ft.
Blu/Gray/White
Streaky Opal

— 3/4 sq. ft. Clear
w/Blk Fractures &
Grn/Pk Streamers

— 1 sq. ft.
Textured
Blue Cath

Vase C
3" (7.6

Reinforce outside perimeter
with a solder bead especially at the
wing & neck joint areas.

The eye is a
glued on solder bead.

PROJECT 6
FLYING DUCK

CUT 1 OF EACH

The apple stems are
heavy gauge copper wire.

PROJECT 3-5
APPLE SERIES

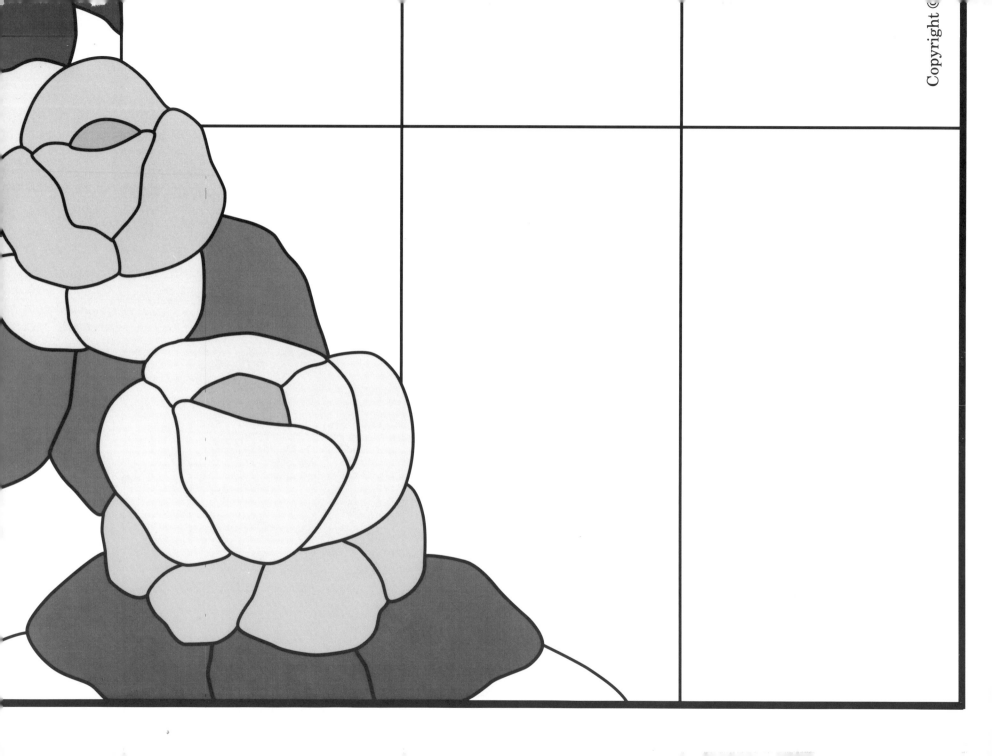

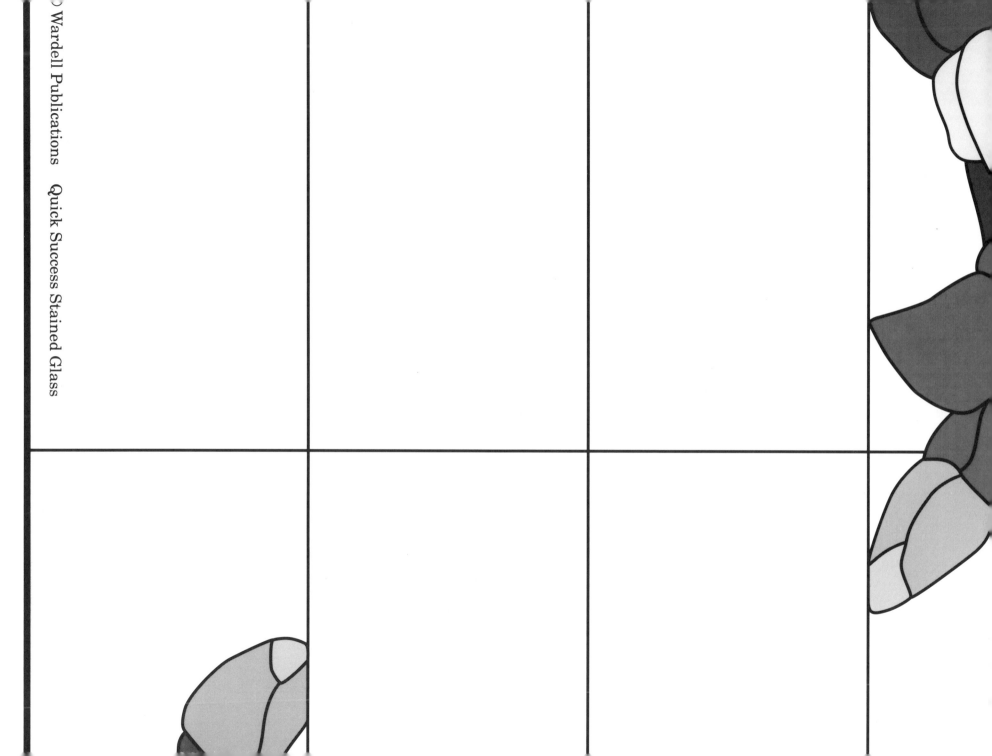

OVAL FLOWER PANEL   PROJECT 10
CUT 1 OF EACH

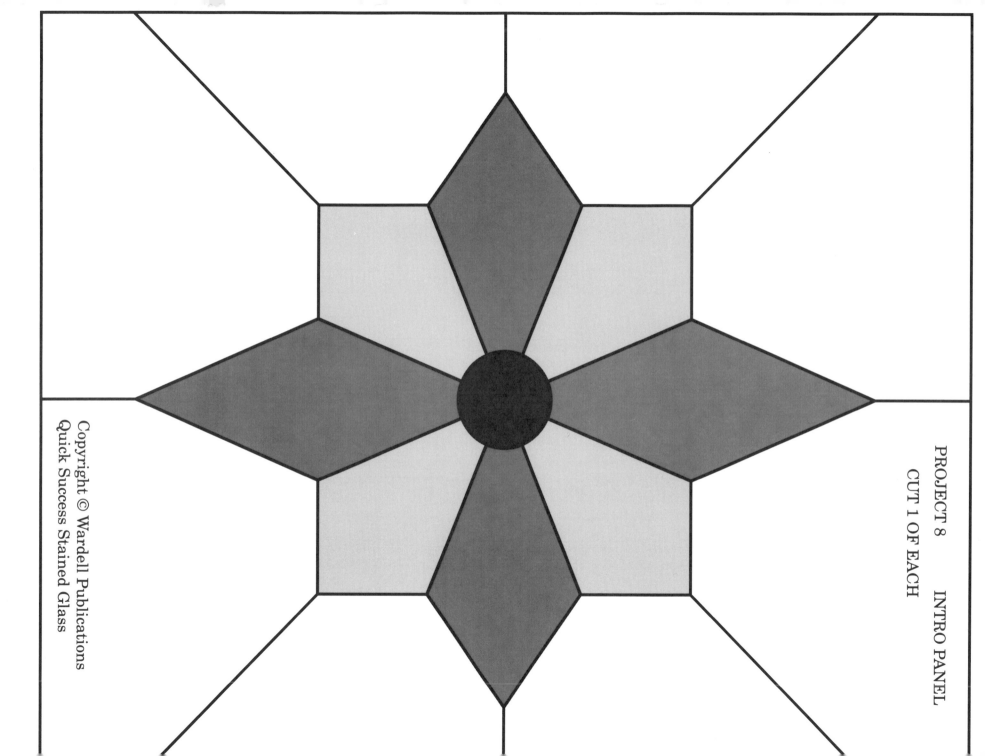

PROJECT 8 INTRO PANEL
CUT 1 OF EACH

PROJECT 13

PROJECT 13   LARGE FLOWER POT

...tern.
CUT 6

Use the solid — lines
for Project 13's pattern.
PROJECT 13   CUT 8

PROJECT 13 BOTTOM
CUT 1

PROJECT 12
BOTTOM
CUT 1

PROJECT 13 BOTTOM
CUT 1

...Y HINT: For Projects 12, 13 & 14.
...ssembly, lay the glass pieces good side down on
...and tape together on the back side of the glass. Pull
...up into a cone (with the tape on the inside of the pot).
...e assembly and bead solder in the same manner as
...de (instructions on page 21).

PROJECT 18   ROSE PANEL

CUT 1 OF EACH

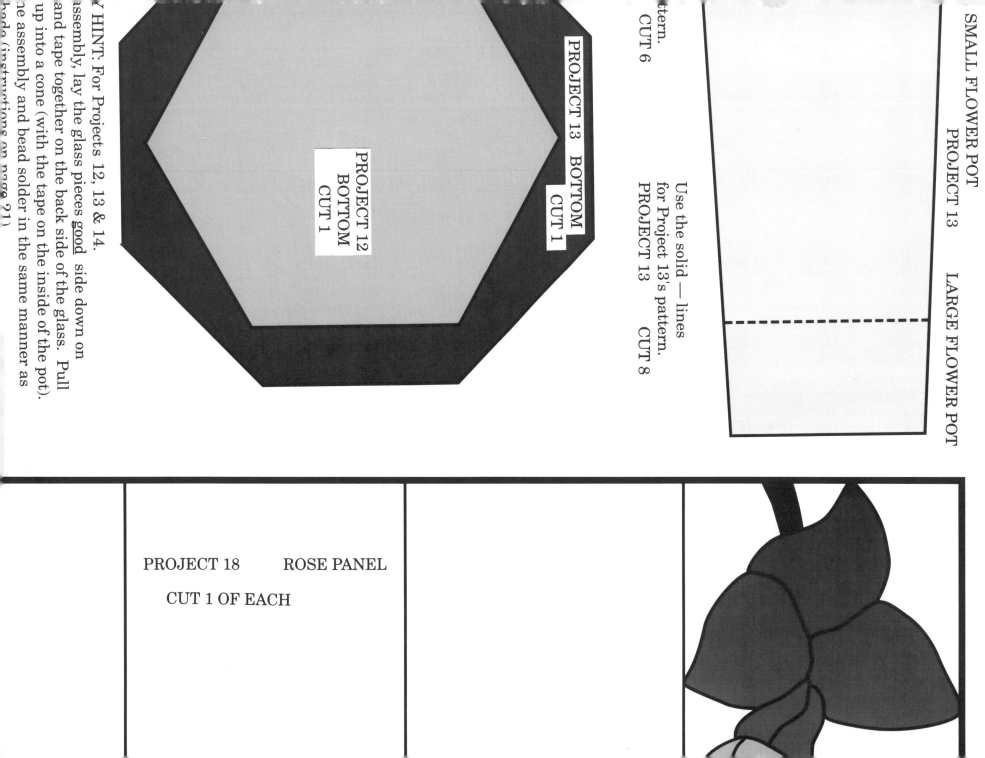

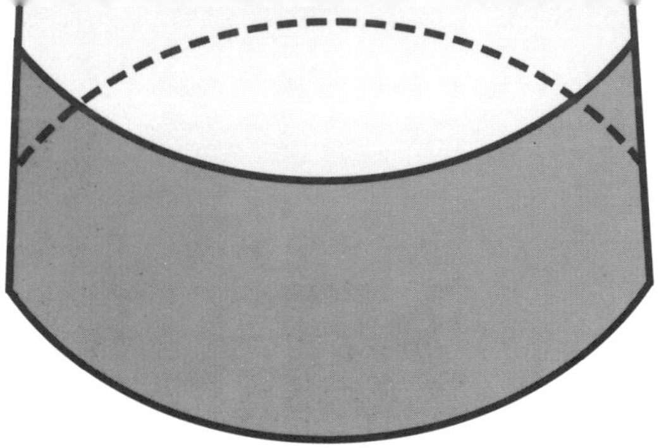

Use the --- lines
for Project 12's pa
PROJECT 12

ASSEMBL
For easier
workboard
the section
Complete t

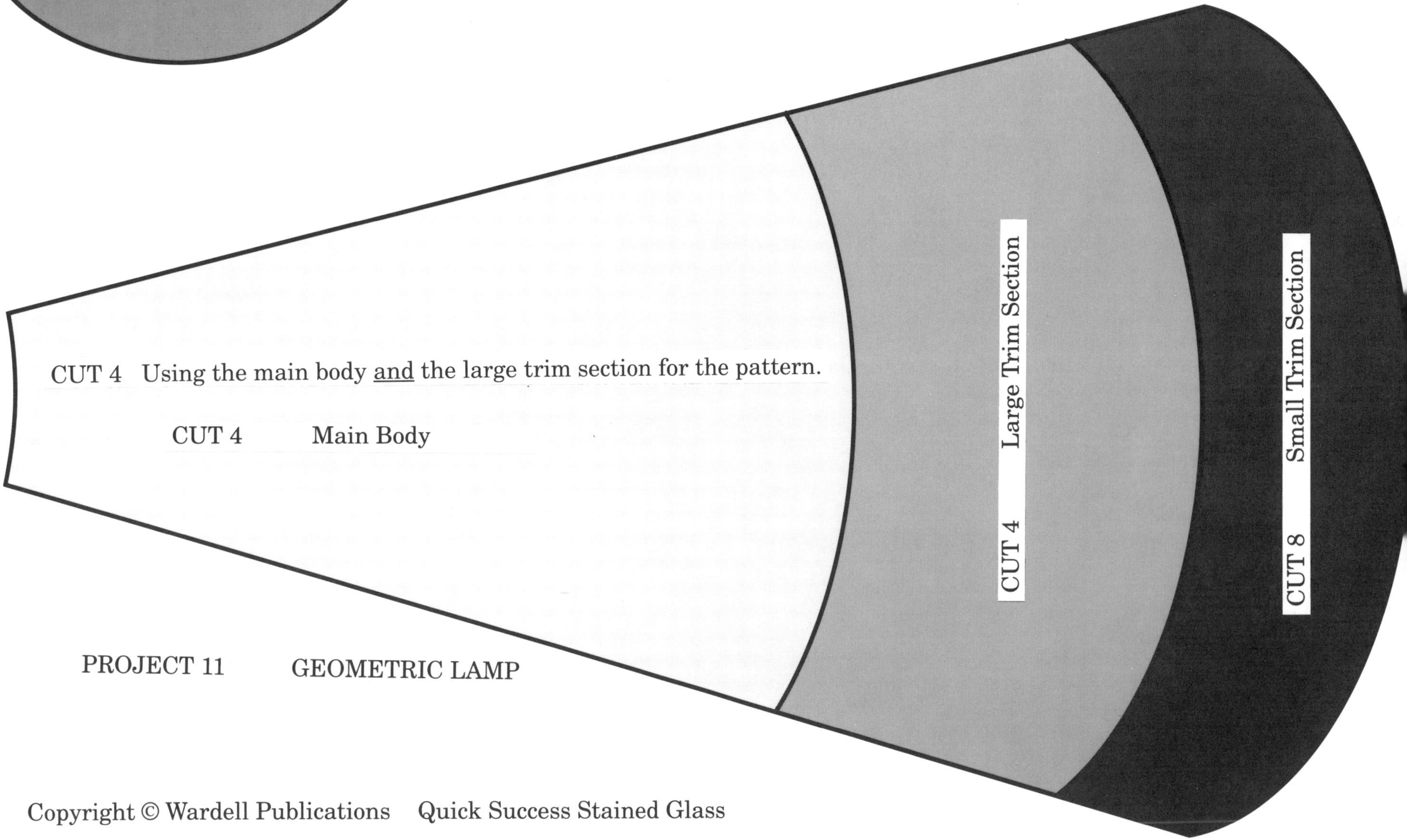

CUT 4   Using the main body <u>and</u> the large trim section for the pattern.

CUT 4   Main Body

Large Trim Section

CUT 4

Small Trim Section

CUT 8

PROJECT 11   GEOMETRIC LAMP

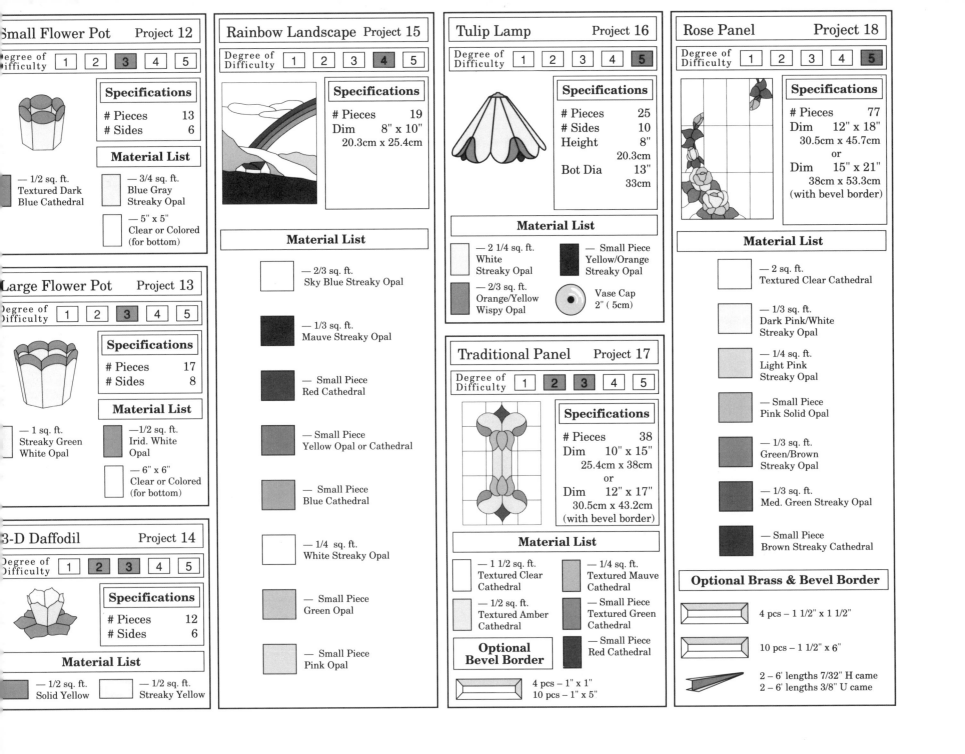

Small Flower Pot — Project 12

Degree of Difficulty: 1 2 **3** 4 5

Specifications
# Pieces	13
# Sides	6

Material List
— 1/2 sq. ft.
Textured Dark
Blue Cathedral

— 3/4 sq. ft.
Blue Gray
Streaky Opal

— 5" x 5"
Clear or Colored
(for bottom)

Large Flower Pot — Project 13

Degree of Difficulty: 1 2 **3** 4 5

Specifications
# Pieces	17
# Sides	8

Material List
— 1 sq. ft.
Streaky Green
White Opal

—1/2 sq. ft.
Irid. White
Opal

— 6" x 6"
Clear or Colored
(for bottom)

3-D Daffodil — Project 14

Degree of Difficulty: 1 **2 3** 4 5

Specifications
# Pieces	12
# Sides	6

Material List
— 1/2 sq. ft.
Solid Yellow

— 1/2 sq. ft.
Streaky Yellow

Rainbow Landscape — Project 15

Degree of Difficulty: 1 2 3 **4** 5

Specifications
# Pieces	19
Dim	8" x 10"
	20.3cm x 25.4cm

Material List
— 2/3 sq. ft.
Sky Blue Streaky Opal

— 1/3 sq. ft.
Mauve Streaky Opal

— Small Piece
Red Cathedral

— Small Piece
Yellow Opal or Cathedral

— Small Piece
Blue Cathedral

— 1/4 sq. ft.
White Streaky Opal

— Small Piece
Green Opal

— Small Piece
Pink Opal

Tulip Lamp — Project 16

Degree of Difficulty: 1 2 3 4 **5**

Specifications
# Pieces	25
# Sides	10
Height	8"
	20.3cm
Bot Dia	13"
	33cm

Material List
— 2 1/4 sq. ft.
White
Streaky Opal

— 2/3 sq. ft.
Orange/Yellow
Wispy Opal

— Small Piece
Yellow/Orange
Streaky Opal

Vase Cap
2" (5cm)

Traditional Panel — Project 17

Degree of Difficulty: 1 **2 3** 4 5

Specifications
# Pieces	38
Dim	10" x 15"
	25.4cm x 38cm
	or
Dim	12" x 17"
	30.5cm x 43.2cm
	(with bevel border)

Material List
— 1 1/2 sq. ft.
Textured Clear
Cathedral

— 1/2 sq. ft.
Textured Amber
Cathedral

— 1/4 sq. ft.
Textured Mauve
Cathedral

— Small Piece
Textured Green
Cathedral

— Small Piece
Red Cathedral

Optional Bevel Border
4 pcs – 1" x 1"
10 pcs – 1" x 5"

Rose Panel — Project 18

Degree of Difficulty: 1 2 3 4 **5**

Specifications
# Pieces	77
Dim	12" x 18"
	30.5cm x 45.7cm
	or
Dim	15" x 21"
	38cm x 53.3cm
	(with bevel border)

Material List
— 2 sq. ft.
Textured Clear Cathedral

— 1/3 sq. ft.
Dark Pink/White
Streaky Opal

— 1/4 sq. ft.
Light Pink
Streaky Opal

— Small Piece
Pink Solid Opal

— 1/3 sq. ft.
Green/Brown
Streaky Opal

— 1/3 sq. ft.
Med. Green Streaky Opal

— Small Piece
Brown Streaky Cathedral

Optional Brass & Bevel Border
4 pcs – 1 1/2" x 1 1/2"

10 pcs – 1 1/2" x 6"

2 – 6' lengths 7/32" H came
2 – 6' lengths 3/8" U came

Soldering Flux; Flux brush; Grinder Fluid; Antique Patinas; Cutter Lubricant.

There are a few consumable items that you will need. Most items are packaged and sold in sufficient quantities to complete several projects.

• Marking Pens:
A medium point black ink marker is necessary to trace the pattern onto most glass, but darker glass will need a special white-paint marker.

From Wardell Publications book
Clock Gallery - 985165

• Solder:
Solder is an alloy (mixture) of metals. It melts at relatively low heat and readily fastens one metal to another. The common

Tin/Lead alloys used in glass crafting are 60/40 (60% tin / 40% lead) 63/37 and 50/50. Generally, either 60/40 or 63/37 is preferred for foil soldering.

Environmental and health safety concerns have prompted the development of a "lead free" solder with properties very similar to the lead solders.

• Flux & Brush:
Flux is necessary to deoxidize (clean) the copper foil and to reduce the surface tension of molten solder. Exercise great care when using flux, as it is a corrosive chemical. Ask for (and read) the Manufacturer Safety Data Sheet (M.S.D.S.) available from your flux supplier.

• Cutter Lubricant:
Follow the manufacturer's recommendation for your glass cutter, or use a water soluble glass cutter lubricant.

Rolls of Foil tape;
Foil Holder / Dispenser

• Copper Foil Tape:
This is very thin sheet-copper with a sticky-tape back. It is wrapped around the outside edges of the glass pieces as a soldering base. Available on a 36 yard roll (33m), in widths from 1/8" (3mm) to 1/2" (13mm).

• Patina:
This chemical is applied to the metal seams of a completed project to change the solder color from silver to antique brass, antique copper, or classic black, depending on the type.

• Standard Clear Glass:
This low cost standard window glass is unquestionably the easiest and most forgiving to cut, making it the best glass for practice scoring. Available in 3/32" (2mm) or 1/8" (3mm) thick.

• Here is a list of the basic supplies you will need. Some of these supplies are specific to the project you choose. For a detailed material listing, please refer to the project specifications chart.

Materials
- Copper foil- 1 roll
- Solder- 1lb. (.5 kg.)
- Flux & Applicator Brush
- Antique Patina
- Cutter Lubricant
- Pattern Paper, Pattern Card, Carbon paper
- Wire- uninsulated 16 gauge
- Black Plastic Electrical Tape
- Standard Clear Glass - 3 square feet (.3m^2)
- Stained Glass - for project, see project specifications
- Glass Cleaner & soft rags

• Wire - uninsulated:
Brass or copper wire (insulation removed) in 14 to 20 gauge.

Glass Cleaner:
Use a commercial glass cleaner (without ammonia), or water mixed with vinegar, dish-soap, or baking soda. To remove flux, special formulas are available.

Glass Scoring and Breaking

- Now the fun begins. You have your tools assembled, a work space set up, some standard clear glass for practice, and a high level of anticipation, so let's get busy!

- But first, read the important safety considerations.

Think About Safety

Safety is a matter of alertness and habit. Knowing how to work safely is only part of the equation. Develop a safety routine before any work session begins.

Check your work area for anything which could cause problems, look for items which might get in your way, and remember the cardinal rule:

A place for everything and everything in its place!

Put on your safety glasses and other safety equipment as necessary. Sweep your cutting board clear of glass chips.

When your safety routine is complete, locate the glass sheet you're going to work on and get ready to lay it on the bench. The following safety rules are very important for handling glass.

Think About Safety

Glass Handling Skills

Always carry glass in a vertical position. Never pick it up or move it in a horizontal (flat) position. A glass sheet can explode under its own weight if held horizontally.

The correct way to pick up and carry a glass sheet is to grasp it with both hands by the top edge or, for a larger (heavier) sheet, pick it up with one hand on the top edge and the other hand supporting the weight on the bottom edge. Never run your hand along a glass edge. Always release your grip to move your hand to a new position.

Just prior to moving a glass sheet, check it for cracks. First, check visually, then lift it slightly and tap the sheet with a finger tip and listen for a crisp *ring.* If you hear a dull *clank,* it has a crack. Do not attempt to move a cracked sheet! Get expert advice.

To place a sheet safely on your work bench, carry it with one hand on the top edge and the other hand on the bottom edge and place the center of the sheet against the bench edge. Then roll or hinge the glass onto the table top, and slide it on fully.

Here are some rules to follow when scoring and breaking glass:
- Wear your safety glasses.
- Stand while scoring.
- Keep your work (the glass) directly in front of you.
- Hold the cutter perpendicular to the surface of the glass.
- Keep the wheel lubricated.
- Never go over a score twice.

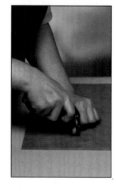

HOLDING THE CUTTER

There are several correct ways to hold a glass cutter. Pictured are three different ways to hold four different cutter varieties. Your instructor or supplier will show you the best way to hold the model you have chosen.

SCORING THE GLASS

Hold the cutter in your favored (tool) hand and place the cutter wheel on the glass about 1/8" (3mm) in from the edge closest to you. Now, place the thumb of your other (guide) hand behind the cutter head to prevent it from rolling back off the glass edge. Apply a firm, constant pressure straight down onto the cutter with your tool hand and push it away from you across the surface of the glass with your guide hand. It will take practice to develop a "feel" for the proper pressure. You should feel the cutter wheel rolling with a slight but even resistance as you slowly progress across the glass. Always score the glass from one edge to another and allow the wheel to roll off the far edge gently. As you score you should also hear a "scritching" noise.

Make an initial score, then carefully examine it. You should see a uniform, pale white line. If the score line appears coarse and gritty, or if small chips are popping from the line, you have exerted too much pressure. Conversely, if the score line is barely visible, you have not applied enough pressure.

NEVER go over the same score twice. Doing so does not improve the score and may damage the cutter wheel.

The pressure required to make a satisfactory score will vary depending on the hardness of the glass. With experience, you will learn to make cutter pressure adjustments as you score.

BREAK OUT THE SCORE

After having made your first score, it is time to run the score. Try to visualize the break as if ripping a piece of cloth. The break starts at one end and should run (follow) along the score line to the other side. The breaking method you use will be influenced by the size, type, and shape of the glass piece to be broken out, as well as by skill

Think About Safety

When breaking out a score, stand with your elbows in close to your sides and always hold the glass over the bench.

When working with larger than 1 sq.ft. (.09 m2) glass pieces, keep one edge resting on the bench.

level and personal choice.

For practice in scoring and breaking, use standard clear glass as listed on page 13. Try shorter length scores at first, as they are generally easier to break out. Continue practicing until you get the feel for scoring and breaking.

Here's a pro tip: It is usually easier to start the break from the finishing end of the score rather than from the glass edge where you started the score.

Breaking with Hands

Form both hands into fists and place the glass between your thumbs and index fingers with the score line between your thumbs. Your fingers should be clenched underneath the glass with knuckles touching. Hold the glass firmly at the end of the score. Apply a quick even "snap" pressure by pulling outward, and roll your knuckles by spreading your thumbs apart.

With Breaker-grozer Pliers

Form one hand into a fist, placing the glass between your thumb and index finger and close to the score line. Position the flat jaw of the breaker-grozer pliers on the top side of the glass with the jaw 90° to the score and as close to the end of the score as possible. Hold the glass firmly in your hand and apply a quick, even pressure by first pulling outward, then snap down with the pliers. Sometimes the glass piece on both sides of the score is too small to hold in your hand. In this case a second pair of pliers would be most helpful.

Glass Scoring and Breaking

• The ability to make a quality score every time is <u>the</u> most important skill a new glass crafter must learn. Practice on standard window glass until you have the *feel* for a successful score. Like learning to ride a bicycle, once you get it, you will never forget the feeling.

• A *quick success* path to score breaking is to use one of the button fulcrum breaking systems. One model uses a pressure block and separate breaker button. Other models are pliers type with the button on the lower jaw. These breakers can be used to run almost any score. The key to their success is the pin-point control of the break, achieved by gently bending the glass over a fulcrum (the button).

• These systems minimize the risk of injury by limiting physical contact with the glass during the breaking.

• More information on the button fulcrum on next page.

Glass Scoring and Breaking

Button Fulcrum Breakers:

These special score-running systems make quick work of breaking out simple shapes and can make otherwise difficult shapes easier. They all operate on the same basic principle. Pressure is applied to the glass directly over a button fulcrum which must be centered over the score. As the break begins to run, the glass (or

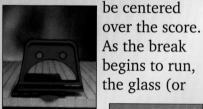

The Morton Safety Break System™

The Glastar Ringstar Pliers™

the fulcrum) is moved along the length of the score, continuously applying pressure, until the glass pieces have separated.

• Ask your stained glass supply shop for a hands-on demonstration of these special breaking tools. They are a handy and welcome addition to many tool boxes.

Button Fulcrum Breaker   *Running Pliers*

Using Running Pliers

Align the guide mark on the top jaw of the running pliers with the score and place the jaws over the glass 1/2" (1 cm) in from the edge. Squeeze firmly on the pliers and the break should run along the score line.

Tapping Under the Score

Sometimes a stubborn score will require some tapping to get the break started. Strike the glass directly under the score with the butt end of your cutter.

From Wardell Publications book
Clock Gallery - 985165

Using a Straight Edge

Position the straight edge along the pattern line, making an allowance for the cutter head. Hold down firmly on the straight edge and start the score at the far end. Pull the cutter toward you, scoring with an even pressure. It is important to keep the cutter perpendicular and parallel to the straight edge.

Breaking a Large Section

To separate a 6" (15cm) or larger strip, score a straight line from one edge to the other. Line up the score with the bench edge. Grasp the glass and raise the end about 2" (5cm) by "hinging" the other end on the bench. Follow through with a firm snap.

Cutting Inside Curves

When tracing a pattern that contains an inside (concave) curve, position the curve as close as possible to the edge of the glass sheet. Score and break out the curve before cutting the piece away from the main sheet.

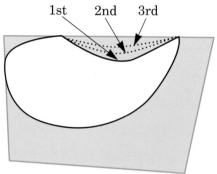

1st   2nd   3rd

First, make the primary score following the inside curve of the pattern. Do not attempt to break this score out yet. Next, make a series of shallow, concave relief scores, starting at one corner and scoring across to the opposite corner (see diagram).

Use breaker-grozer pliers to grasp one end of the outside piece and break it out. Continue breaking out the relief scores in sequence until the inside curve is complete.

Cutting Circles & Ovals

First, score completely around the primary pattern line. Next, make several relief lines tangent to the primary score line on the circle or oval. Using pliers, break away all the relief pieces.

PATTERN MAKING

Today, glass crafters have thousands of stained glass designs available as full-size patterns (18 are included in this book). These designs are full-size, complete and ready to use. However, you still need to create the actual glass cutting templates and the assembly drawing. This is done quite simply by tracing two copies of the original design. Using carbon paper, trace one on standard paper (like the pages of this book) and one on heavy pattern card (like the cover of this book).

First, lay the pattern card on your workboard, followed by carbon paper, standard paper, another carbon, and finally the original design drawing. Secure this assembly with tape or push-pins and carefully trace the drawing, pressing firmly. After being traced, each piece must be numbered to keep track of your pattern pieces. You may want to code them according to your color selections, eg. B1-B8 for blue,

R9-R15 for red, etc. You should also mark the desired direction of the glass streaks on the pattern (if applicable). When you have completed these steps, set aside all pattern copies except the heavier card copy.

The final step is to cut the pattern card into the actual templates for glass cutting. To do this you must consider the method of construction. Copper foil assembly requires an allowance of 1/32" (1mm) between each glass piece to make room for the foil and solder. Came assembly would require an allowance of 3/32" (2mm). The best way to make this allowance is to actually remove a 1/32" (1mm) strip of paper while cutting the pattern by using special foil pattern shears. The alternative (and more difficult) method is to cut the patterns with standard scissors or a craft knife, and make the necessary allowance while cutting and fitting the glass pieces.

CUTTING TO A PATTERN

Use a medium point marker to trace around the pattern template and transfer the exact shape onto the colored glass.

Now, carefully score the glass following along the <u>inside</u> of the traced line, not down the middle. In other words, you must *cut the marker line away,* so the line is left on the waste glass when you break it off. By removing the line, the glass piece will be exactly the same size as the original pattern template.

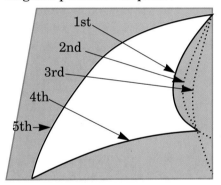

The above diagram illustrates the ideal scoring sequence for a typical project piece. Remember to score and break out the inside curve before moving on.

Periodically check the accuracy of your scoring by placing the pattern template back on top of the cut-out glass piece. Make adjustments as you move on to score the next piece.

• There are several correct ways to use full-size pattern templates to cut glass pieces accurately. However, many instructors agree that the trace & cut method is the most versatile and easiest to learn. You may choose to investigate the other options later on, but trace & cut will always serve your needs.

• For quick success, be sure to get a quality pair of foil pattern shears. They take the guess-work out of pattern making and add a slight margin for scoring errors.

From Wardell Publications book
Wall Decorations - 985033

Here we go! The theory is over, the basics are complete. You are about to begin your stained glass apprenticeship.

Here in point form are the steps to complete your first foil assembly project.

• Make two carbon copies of the project drawing, then cut out the pattern templates using special foil shears.

• Trace patterns onto the glass, score the pieces and break them out.

• Build the assembly jig, then place and fit all your glass pieces on the drawing.

• Clean, wrap & burnish each glass piece with the foil tape.

• Flux and flat solder all foil seams on both front and back side of panel. Finish by bead soldering all seams.

• Place panel in a wood or metal frame.

• Clean thoroughly, patina (if desired) and ENJOY!

Your First Foiled Project Pattern is on center insert page.

THE FOIL METHOD

The foil display at your glass supply store will be overflowing with a vast array of choices. You will find foils of different widths, thicknesses, colors, fancy shaped edges, and so on. Each choice has its specialized use, but for now we will deal only with the standard copper foil.

Stained glass foil has a sticky-tape back that must be centered and wrapped around the outside edge of each piece of glass. The width of the foil used must be matched to the thickness of the glass being wrapped, to allow a minimum 1/32" (1mm) overhang that is folded down onto both the top and bottom glass surfaces. The three most common foil widths are 3/16" (5mm), 7/32" (5.5mm), and 1/4" (6.2mm). New crafters usually find a wider foil easier to work with. Ask your instructor or supplier for their foil recommendation.

Trace the pattern templates, score & break the glass & check for accuracy.

Trace and Cut

Trace one of your pattern templates onto the selected glass with a marker, remembering to transfer the code number. Cut that glass piece out by scoring on the inside of the line and check it to the pattern for accuracy. Continue scoring and breaking until all pieces are cut out.

Assembly Jig

Build an assembly jig with wood trim and nails or use the Layout Block System™. Fasten it along the outside line of your working drawing. Arrange all your glass pieces on the drawing inside the jig. Some pieces will require grozing or grinding to make them fit properly.

The assembly jig with project pieces in place. Some will need fitting.

Fitting and Shaping

Starting with a corner glass piece, compare its shape carefully with the lines on the working drawing. Mark all areas that are over the line with your marker, then take that piece to the grinder and selectively remove the extra glass. Place the piece back into the jig, position an adjacent piece, mark the areas which are oversize, grind and replace it. Position the next adjacent piece, mark, grind and so on until all pieces fit as accurately as possible. The fit

Marking the oversized areas & grinding the selections on the glass grinder.

should be a little loose inside the jig at this point; remember, there must be room for two layers of foil between each piece. If the fit is too tight, you will find that the pieces won't go back into the jig after foil wrapping.

Foil Wrapping

Before starting the foil wrapping process, each piece of glass (and your hands) must be meticulously cleaned. Cutter oil, grinding residue, even your own finger prints will adversely affect the foil adhesive.

Pull a length of foil tape from the roll and peel back 2" (5cm) of the protective paper backing. Hold the glass vertical, so you can sight down both sides. Press the sticky end of the foil firmly onto the glass edge, leaving exactly the same amount of overhang on either side. Peel slightly more backing, move further along the piece and press the foil to the edge, peel more backing and press, peel and

Center the foil by sighting down both sides of the glass. Fold & crimp edges.

press firmly as you continue around the glass perimeter. When you get back to the starting point, cut or tear the foil, leaving enough length to overlap the two ends at least 1/4" (6mm). Crimp (fold) the foil down over the glass edges with your thumb and index finger by pinching and pressing toward the center. When crimping an inside curve, press slowly to avoid splitting the foil; if it does split, simply add a foil patch long enough to cover the area.

Wrap and crimp all glass pieces in the project.

Finally, burnish the foil tightly against the glass on both front and back sides to ensure that the foil does not pull away from the glass. Using the rounded edge of your lathekin (fid), press down and toward the center of the glass piece, paying close attention to corners and inside curves. When all pieces have been foiled and burnished smooth, place them back into the assembly jig where they should be snug but not bulging. Do a final quality check and make any last minute adjustments.

SOLDERING

All foiled joints must be completely soldered (not just at the corners) to create the metal web which will hold the panel together. You will need your

soldering iron, flux, and solder.

Flat Soldering

Soldering begins by brushing flux on the foil seams. Now, with the hot soldering iron in one hand and solder in the other, place the wider, flat side of the iron tip directly on a foil seam and touch the solder to the top surface of the iron tip. The solder will immediately melt and coat the foil under the iron tip.

Flat soldering all seams with the wide flat side of a hot iron tip.

Move the iron slowly along the seam, continuously adding more solder, filling gaps and covering the foil as you go. This process is referred to as "flat soldering". When you have flat soldered all top seams, remove the layout assembly jig, turn your project over and flat solder the back side.

From Wardell Publications book
Introduction to Stained Glass - 985041

Once both sides of the panel have been flat soldered it will be solid enough to hold up to the light for a little well deserved gratification.

Think About Safety

- Wear safety glasses when cutting, grinding and soldering.
- Flux is a corrosive chemical and may irritate skin. Wear rubber gloves to protect hands.
- Avoid inhaling soldering fumes; provide adequate ventilation by setting up a fan to pull fumes away from your face.

Bead Soldering

The finishing touch is called bead soldering. The idea is to build up solder on the seams until it forms a rounded bead.

Running a solder bead with the iron tip vertical and side feeding the solder.

Re-flux the flat soldered seams just prior to bead soldering.

Place the iron on a flat soldered joint, parallel to the seam, with the chisel side of the tip vertical (opposite to flat soldering). Pull the iron steadily along the seam, continuously feeding solder to the tip. As you move the iron along, keep an eye on the bead as it forms at the tip. If the bead is too flat, slow down and add more solder; if the bead bulges and overflows, add less solder. If the bead forms and then disappears, your moving too slowly and the solder has melted through to the other side. Don't worry, just move on, let that section cool, and come back to it later.

Turn the project over and completely solder the back side. All exposed foil must be coated with solder, including the outer edge. Clean the panel with glass cleaner and a soft rag.

If you plan to hang your project in a window as an autonomous (independent) panel it should be installed in a wood or metal frame. Wire loops soldered to the foil-only edge will not be strong enough to hold the weight over a long period of time.

Patina

To get the best possible color result, apply the patina solution immediately after soldering.

Use caution; patina is a corrosive chemical. Wear rubber gloves and carefully follow the safety instructions on the patina container and in the M.S.D.S.

From Wardell Publications book
Designs For Lamps - 985068

Foiled project with optional beveled glass border added using brass came.

METAL CAME BORDER

The project shown above has had a bevel border added using solid brass came. Metal came is manufactured from lead, brass, zinc or copper and is shaped into U (outer) or H (inner) channels. The assembly method is similar for all metal cames.

Cut the pattern pieces using *came* shears (see pg. 12) for all lines where you plan to use the metal came. Cut the remainder of the pattern using foil shears. Assemble, solder and clean the foiled center section as described on pages 18 to 20.

Nail two pieces of glazing trim (or layout strips) at 90° on one corner of the working drawing, making an allowance for the metal came. Next, cut two pieces of outer U came, one for the side, one for the bottom, and lay them on the drawing along the trim. Fit the first glass piece into the

corner channels and use a hammer and wood block to seat it with a gentle tap. Secure the glass with a nail or push-pin and a scrap piece of came. Make sure the glass edges are inside the drawing lines; if not, grind and fit before moving on.

Fitting the first corner piece .   *Inserting the center section.*

Position some of the H channel along one edge of the glass piece and mark its length for cutting, being sure to allow for the adjoining channel depth. Cut the channel with a came saw and place it in the assembly. Fit the next glass piece, tack with a nail, measure and cut the next came, and so on until the bottom and side borders are complete.

Remove some of the tack nails and place the foiled center section into the came assembly. Now secure it with tack nails, and finish the rest of the border in a similar manner.

Complete by soldering all joints, (including the foil seams), for both front and back sides.

A FOILED LAMPSHADE

Trace the working drawing and pattern template in the usual manner, using foil shears for all interior design lines.

Score and break out all glass pieces. Build an assembly jig, place and fit glass pieces and code number each individual set. Foil and burnish the edges of all pieces. Place pieces back into the jig, one set at a time, and solder them together. Complete each section with a finish solder bead. Do not solder the outside edges.

Be sure to thoroughly clean the flux residue from each panel, or the assembly tape will not stick.

Cut, fit and solder each lampshade panel in an assembly jig.

Tape assembled panels in a semi circle and raise it up into a cone shape.

Lay the panels on your bench, face side up, to form a semi-circle in the correct sequence. Tape the sections together using black plastic electrical tape. Carefully grasp the small diameter center and raise this row up into a cone, always keeping the large diameter end on the bench. Bring the two adjoining side sections together and tape. Keep the bottom of the cone flat on the bench and secure around the base with nails or push pins.

Solder each joint at the bottom and as much of the exposed outside seam as possible. Fit and solder the vase cap to the top of the lampshade.

Tack solder each bottom joint and solder the vase cap into the top opening.

Remove the nails or push pins and turn the shade upside down in a cardboard box filled with loosely crumpled newspapers. Solder all inside seams and around the vase cap.

If your lampshade project has any glass joiner pieces, they must be inserted at this time.

Place the lampshade in a soldering box and flat solder all inside seams.

Now, turn the lamp right side up in the soldering box and remove some of the black tape.

Position the lamp in the box so the seam that you intend to solder is level. Take your time and run a bead of solder. If the molten solder is flowing away from the iron tip, this indicates that the seam is not perfectly level and you must reposition the lamp. If you have to fill a gap and the molten solder drips through, cover the space from the inside with masking tape.

Level the lampshade in the soldering box and bead solder all outside seams.

Constructing a Foiled Lampshade

• Three dimensional project constructions are somewhat more difficult than flat items. Please, do not attempt a lampshade or planter until you have gained some basic cutting, fitting, assembly, and soldering experience.

Finish the bottom edge with a solder bead or solder a 14 gauge wire completely around the bottom edge for reinforcement.

Clean the shade thoroughly and patina if desired.

The completed Lampshade. Pattern is on center insert page.

Tricks, Hints and Troubleshooting

• Learning the *tricks of the trade* from an expert is a proven key to quick success. The following section contains answers to some of the most common difficulties encountered by new stained glass crafters.

• Tricks of the trade are marked in *italic lettering* for easy reference throughout the troubleshooting hints.

From Wardell Publications book
Mirrors & Frames - 985157

SCORING & BREAKING

You think you've made a good score, but it just won't break out successfully. First, don't rely on the "sound" to judge a quality score. Some glass types make very faint sounds, or none at all. Second, it is very easy to make a "false score" when using a straight edge. Many times, the cutter is turned into the guide, producing a scratch instead of a score. Third, the ideal cutter pressure can vary greatly from one glass to another. Learn to "feel" the cutter wheel rolling with a slight but even resistance. Here are some other things to take into account.

• **Scoring Considerations:**
-too much scoring pressure.
-too little scoring pressure.
-cutter was not held at 90° (perpendicular) to glass surface.
-too little or no cutter fluid.
-cutter jumped over a bump or bubble, creating a skip. *When the cutter wheel hits a bump or falls into a bubble hole, nudge the cutter head along with the thumb on your guide hand.*
-score was made on the wrong (back) side of the glass sheet.
-cutter wheel is dull, chipped or seized in its housing.

• **Breaking Considerations:**
-remember to pull apart, then snap down when breaking by hand or with pliers.
- break from the widest end and run toward the narrowest end. *Start the break from the finishing end of a score.*
-not enough secondary relief scores for the deep inside curve.
-waited too long to break out and score has become cold.

FOIL PROBLEMS

• **Foil doesn't stick very well to edge when wrapping:**
-glass edges must be very clean before foil wrapping. *Wash pieces in hot water and dish soap or diluted denatured alcohol.*
-make sure your hands are clean, and keep fingers off the sticky tape back.
Foil will stick better to slightly warmed up glass pieces. Set them in the sun or use a hand-held hair dryer just prior to foiling.
-old foil can loose its sticking power. *Store foil in a cool place and keep it in a zip-lock plastic bag to avoid oxidization.*

• **Foil pulls away from edge during or after soldering:**
-glass was not clean enough prior to wrapping.
-foil was not burnished tightly to the glass after wrapping.
-edges often require a bead of solder to hold the foil in place, especially inside curves.

• **Foil overlap joint pulled apart on outside edge:**
When foil wrapping, position the overlap joint on a side that will become an inside seam.

SOLDERING PROBLEMS

It takes many hours of practice to consistently produce a quality solder bead. Have patience with yourself. Consider the following.

• **Solder won't stick to foil:**
-area was not fluxed.
-foil may be oxidized; buff with fine (000) steel wool.

• **Solder will not flow; bead has points, peaks or ripples:**
-area was not fluxed.
-wrong type of flux used.
-wrong alloy of solder used.
-iron may be too cold or tip may be loose in barrel.

From Wardell Publications book
Classic Alphabets - 985130

From Wardell Publications book
Terrariums & Planters - 985025

• **Iron seems hot, but is slower than usual or won't melt the solder at all:**

-tip may be loose in iron barrel

-tip may be dirty; use a damp iron cleaner sponge.

-tip may be corroded and needs to be replaced.

-iron temperature control mechanism is malfunctioning.

• **Soldered seams are flat:**

-not enough solder; re-flux and add more solder.

• **Soldered seams are wide:**

-foil was too wide for the thickness of glass used.

-glass fit was too loose, leaving gaps between glass pieces.

• **Soldered seams are irregular in widths:**

- glass fit was sloppy leaving too many large gaps.

- foil was not carefully centered when wrapped. *Use a craft knife to trim and straighten excess foil just prior to soldering.*

• **Rough or uneven bead:**

-moving iron too quickly.

-iron may be too cool.

-let the solder flow; don't try to spread it on. *The key is to get the solder just hot enough to take advantage of the physics of fluids. Control the spot temperature by touching the iron tip in and out until the ripples are gone.*

• **Hot solder drips down through seam:**

-iron is too hot or is being held in one spot for too long.

-there is an open gap between the glass pieces. *Stick a piece of masking tape down the backside of the seam to hold the hot solder up; very useful when bead soldering lampshades.*

• **Glass suddenly cracked during soldering:**

-heat fractures are caused by excessive heating of the glass. Your iron may be too hot, or you may have been working in one area for too long.

• **Solder bead has dull, uneven blotchy areas:**

-these "cold" solder areas were not sufficiently heated; your iron may be too cool.

-may require more flux or a different type.

• **Solder spits and splatters:**

-liquid flux has pooled in some gaps; apply less generously.

-iron may be too hot and is boiling the flux.

PATTERN PROBLEMS

• **Pattern shears keep getting jammed, especially on tight curves:**

-use short strokes and take small bites as you move along the pattern lines.

You will encounter less shear jamming if you lubricate the blades with a light coating of no-stick cooking spray.

• **Assembly drawings get wet, become ragged, and can only be used once:**

If you intend to save a design for possible future use, protect the assembly drawing with an adhesive-backed clear vinyl sheet. Cover prior to glass grinding and fitting.

• **Using a photocopier to make the pattern:**

-a photocopier can be used to tremendous advantage when making your pattern copies. Zoom photocopiers can be used to enlarge or reduce the drawing size according to your needs. But be warned, photocopiers are not perfect, since they often distort the original drawing. This may not be a problem for most flat or free-form projects, but even a slight variance can be disastrous for lampshade patterns. Be sure to compare photocopies to the original for all your patterns.

• While you have come to the end of this instruction book, you have only begun to experience the wealth of knowledge available in the stained glass industry. There are hundreds of pattern books, several magazines, dozens of videos, and numerous instructional courses available to you. Also, just down the street at your local stained glass shop, you will find some of the most excited, friendly, and willing-to-share folks you will ever meet. Get to know these people and don't be afraid to ask them questions. They can guide you through any glass problem. They are a resource; use them!

From Wardell Publications book
Lampworks - 985149

Wardell
PUBLICATIONS INC

e-mail: info@wardellpublications.com – website: www.wardellpublications.com

WINDOWS FOR THE SOUL
Ecclesiastic art glass at Bovard Studio
RON BOVARD

Stu Goldman's
9x9 Lives
Cat Designs
Project Book
9 Adaptations of 9 Patterns
A Total of 81 Projects
Skill Level - Beginner to Advanced

Stained Glass
Windows of Vision
Collection Four
Featuring
Leslie Perlis Studio

Stained Glass
Windows of Elegance
Collection Two
STUDIO DESIGNERS

NORTHERN SHADES

DESIGNS FOR LAMPS II
Patterns For 8 Small
Charles Knapp

DESIGNS FOR LAMPS
Patterns for 18 Small to Medium

INTRODUCTION TO
STAINED GLASS
A TEACHING MANUAL

QUICK SUCCESS
STAINED GLASS
A BEGINNER'S INSTRUC...
Wardell

Stained Glass
Windows of Distinction
Collection One
McMow Art Glass
STUDIO DESIGNERS

Stained Glass
Windows of North America
Collection Three

LAMPSHADE PATTERNS I
MORE
LAMPSHADE PATTERNS
FOR MINI TO MEDIUM SH...

LAMPSHADE PATTERNS II
CHARLES KNAPP

LAMPWORKS

INITIATION
AU VITR...
Guide d'...

Introducción
AL VITR...
Manual

Classic Alphabets
FULL SIZED ALPHABETS

STAINED GLASS
Clock Gallery

STAINED GLASS
WALL DECORATIONS
PATTERNS FOR CLOCKS,
MIRRORS AND PICTURE FRAM...

ART GLASS
INSPIRAT...
by SUE CANN
STAINED GLASS

MIRRORS
& FRAM...
PATTERNS FOR

Bevel Window Designs
CREATIVE INSPIRATIONS FOR LEADED
STAINED GLASS WINDOWS

TERRARIUMS
& PLANT...
PATTERNS FOR

Stained Glass
BOXES